DELIGHTFUL
DECIMALS AND
PERFECT PERCENTS

Also in the Magical Math series

Magical Math

DELIGHTFUL DECIMALS AND PERFECT PERCENTS

Games and Activities That Make Math Easy and Fun

Lynette Long

John Wiley & Sons, Inc.

10 9 8 7 6 5 4 3 2 1

Contents

~~~ 1 ~~~

THE MAGIC OF DECIMALS AND PERCENTS

Decimals and percents are everywhere. If you go to the grocery store, you'll find the cost of everything expressed in decimals. The weight of the meat is also expressed in decimals. And if there is a sale on meat, it might be expressed as a percent. If you want to succeed at math and really understand the world you live in, you have to get to know decimals and percents.

But what are decimals? Like fractions, decimals are numbers that represent part of a whole, but unlike fractions, decimals don't use a fraction bar. Instead they use a decimal point. Everything to the right of the decimal point is less than zero, and everything to the left of the decimal point is greater than zero. One thing that makes decimals easy to work with is that, unlike fractions, you don't have to find a common denominator to add or subtract them.

You will use decimals and percents every day of your life. So you might as well start practicing. Begin with the fun activities in this book and you'll soon be a master of decimals and percents. Then you can proudly display the decimals and percents master certificate at the back of this book.

THE FACTS ON DECIMALS

In this section, you'll learn all the basic facts about decimals. You'll learn how to read a decimal and write one, how to change a decimal to a percent, and, of course, how to change a fraction to a decimal and a decimal to a fraction. Last but not least, you'll learn what a repeating decimal is. While learning, you'll solve a decimal dot-to-dot, check out the stats of your favorite baseball team on the Internet, and play some fast-paced games with your friends.

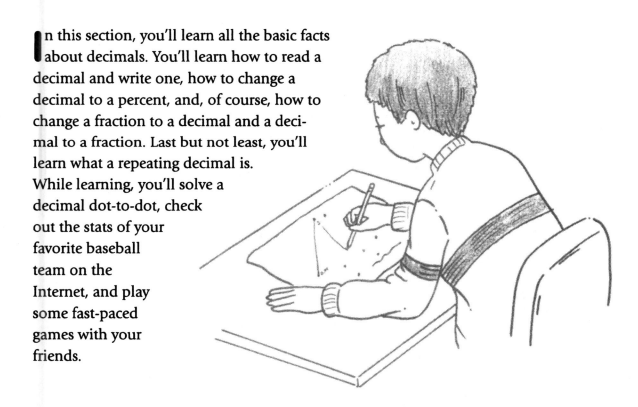

Scavenger Hunt

Fractions, decimals, and percents express parts of wholes. In fact, you can use fractions, decimals, and percents to describe parts of just about anything. The statements "³/5 of Americans prefer chocolate ice cream over vanilla," "0.6 of Americans prefer chocolate ice cream over vanilla," and "60% of Americans prefer chocolate ice cream over vanilla" all mean the same thing. Which version you use depends partly on convention (what other people do in the same situation) and partly on practicality (it's easier to say "two-thirds" than "0.666666666 . . ."). In this game, you'll compete with friends to find examples of fractions, decimals, and percents in a newspaper.

MATERIALS

2 or more players
several sheets of white paper
pencils
old newspapers
scissors
glue

Game Preparation

1. Each player should fold a piece of white paper into eight sections. Write one of the following fractions at the top of each section:

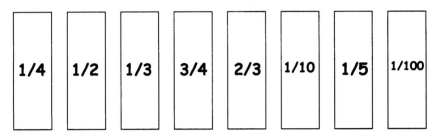

2. Each player should fold a second piece of white paper into eight sections. Write one of the following decimals in each section:

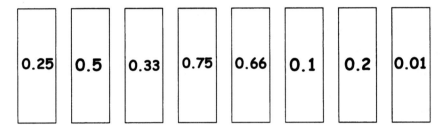

3. Each player should fold a third sheet of white paper into eight sections. Write one of the following percents in each section.

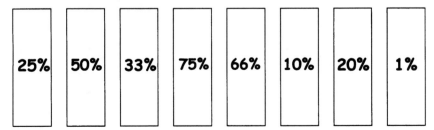

Game Rules

1. Each player should take a stack of newspapers. Players have 30 minutes to look through the newspapers and to cut out and glue on their sheets examples of any of the listed fractions, decimals, and percents.

2. After the 30 minutes are up, players should count the numbers of fractions, decimals, and percents on their sheets. The player who has the most wins the scavenger hunt.

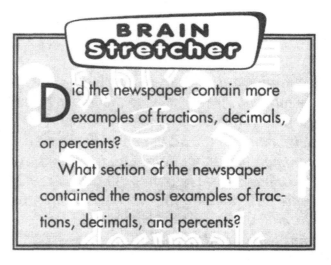

BRAIN Stretcher

Did the newspaper contain more examples of fractions, decimals, or percents?

What section of the newspaper contained the most examples of fractions, decimals, and percents?

Name That Place!

The value of a numeral depends on its place in the number. Look at any number. As you move to the left, every place is 10 times larger than the previous place. As you move to the right, every place is one-tenth the place on its left. Here are the values of common places: millions, hundred-thousands, ten-thousands, hundreds, tens, ones, (DECIMAL POINT) tenths, hundredths, thousandths, ten-thousandths, hundred-thousandths, millionths. Notice that the decimal point separates the numerals that are greater than one from the numerals that are less than one. Learn the value of decimal numbers with this fast-paced game.

MATERIALS

2 players
10 index cards
pencil
die
stopwatch or watch with second hand

Game Preparation

1. Write one of these numbers on each index card.

100,200,345.6	65.4321
3,040,500,126	0.213645
3,456.12	102,030.40506
2.65431	123.456
60.12345	6,543.0201

Game Rules

1. Shuffle the index cards and turn them facedown in front of player 1.

2. Player 1 rolls the die. The number rolled is the *Name That Place!* number.

3. Player 2 starts the stopwatch and gives player 1 one minute to *Name That Place!* on the entire stack of 10 cards.

4. Player 1 turns over the top card. He or she looks at the decimal on the top card and names the place in which the rolled number appears in the place in the card.

   Example: If the number on the card is 123.456 and the rolled number is 6, then the player shouts "Thousandths!." If the rolled number is 5, the player shouts "Hundredths!." If the rolled number is 4, the player shouts "Tenths!" and so on.

5. Player 1 turns over the rest of the cards one by one and repeats step 4 for each card. *Note:* The rolled number stays the same through each player's turn. Each player only rolls the die once.

6. If player 1 names all 10 place values correctly, he or she wins one point.

7. If a player names a place value incorrectly, he or she loses the rest of his or her turn.

8. After player 1's turn is over, the index cards are shuffled and placed facedown in front of player 2.

9. Player 2 rolls the die to get a new *Name That Place!* number. Player 2 now has one minute to see if he or she can *Name That Place!* for the same 10 index cards. If player 2 is successful, he or she earns one point. Player 1 sets the timer for this turn.

10. Players alternate turns at *Name That Place!* until one player gets five points. That player is the winner.

Tips and Tricks

Draw a chart like this one. Enter your decimal numbers into the chart and use the top row of the chart to help you read them.

Thousands	Hundreds	Tens	Ones	DECIMAL POINT	Tenths	Hundredths	Thousandths

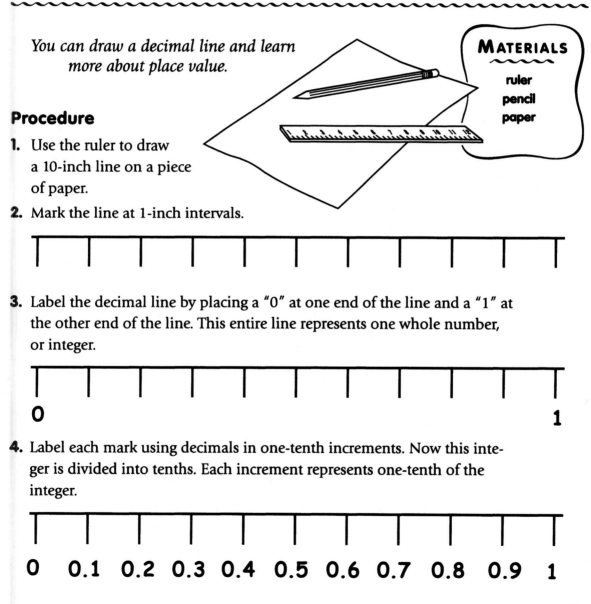

3 Decimals on the Line

You can draw a decimal line and learn more about place value.

MATERIALS

ruler
pencil
paper

Procedure

1. Use the ruler to draw a 10-inch line on a piece of paper.

2. Mark the line at 1-inch intervals.

3. Label the decimal line by placing a "0" at one end of the line and a "1" at the other end of the line. This entire line represents one whole number, or integer.

0   1

4. Label each mark using decimals in one-tenth increments. Now this integer is divided into tenths. Each increment represents one-tenth of the integer.

0   0.1   0.2   0.3   0.4   0.5   0.6   0.7   0.8   0.9   1

5. Make a mark halfway between each two decimal numbers. Label these marks 0.05, 0.15, 0.25, 0.35, 0.45, 0.55, 0.65, 0.75, 0.85, and 0.95.

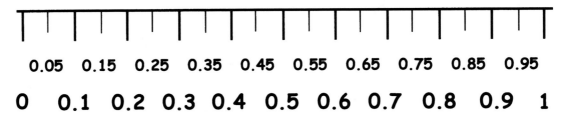

| 0.05 | 0.15 | 0.25 | 0.35 | 0.45 | 0.55 | 0.65 | 0.75 | 0.85 | 0.95 |

| 0 | 0.1 | 0.2 | 0.3 | 0.4 | 0.5 | 0.6 | 0.7 | 0.8 | 0.9 | 1 |

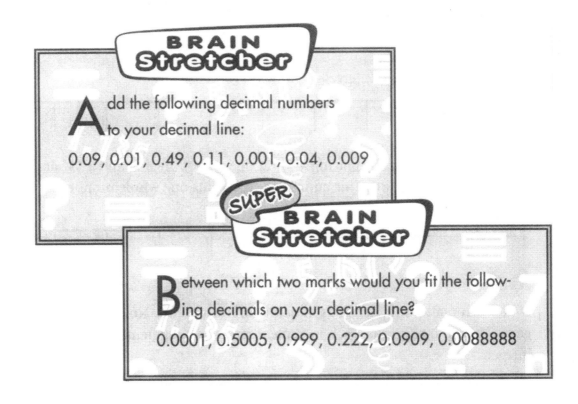

BRAIN Stretcher

Add the following decimal numbers to your decimal line:

0.09, 0.01, 0.49, 0.11, 0.001, 0.04, 0.009

SUPER BRAIN Stretcher

Between which two marks would you fit the following decimals on your decimal line?

0.0001, 0.5005, 0.999, 0.222, 0.0909, 0.0088888

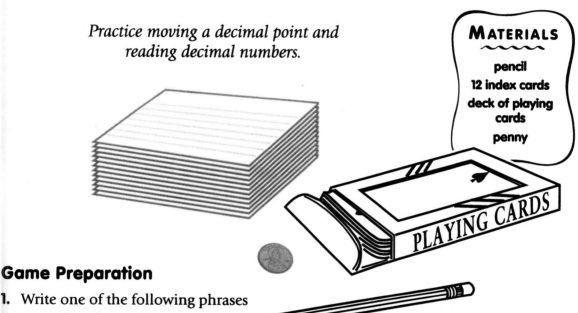

Roving Decimal Points

Practice moving a decimal point and reading decimal numbers.

MATERIALS

pencil

12 index cards

deck of playing cards

penny

Game Preparation

1. Write one of the following phrases on each index card:

    Move the decimal point two places to the right.

    Move the decimal point two places to the right.

    Move the decimal point two places to the left.

    Move the decimal point two places to the left.

    Move the decimal point one place to the right.

    Move the decimal point one place to the right.

    Move the decimal point one place to the left.

    Move the decimal point one place to the left.

Move the decimal point three places to the right.

Move the decimal point three places to the left.

Keep the decimal point in the same place.

Keep the decimal point in the same place.

2. Remove the face cards (kings, queens, and jacks) from a deck of playing cards. These picture cards will be used to represent zeros.

Game Rules

1. Shuffle the index cards and place them facedown on the table.

2. Shuffle the numbered playing cards and place them facedown on the table.

3. Turn over the top three playing cards. Place them in a row on the table. Using the penny as a decimal point, place the decimal point to the right of all three cards. Read this number. Aces are the same as ones.

4. Turn over the top index card. Move the decimal point (penny) according to the direction on the card. Use the picture cards as zeros to fill in any empty spaces. What is the new decimal number?

5. Continue to turn over the top index card. Keep moving the decimal point (penny) according to the directions on each card. Use the picture cards as zeros to fill in any empty spaces. Read each new number out loud. Keep playing until you've gone through all the index cards.

6. Put your first three playing cards aside. Take out three more cards from the deck. Reshuffle the index cards and play again! What is the largest number you created? What is the smallest number you created?

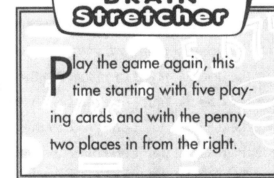

BRAIN Stretcher

Play the game again, this time starting with five playing cards and with the penny two places in from the right.

Tips and Tricks

Read the decimal point as "AND." If the decimal is less than one, put a zero in the ones place. Don't forget to name that place, whether it's tenths, hundredths, or thousandths.

Examples:

1.23 is read as one and twenty-three hundredths.

0.007 is read as zero and seven-thousandths.

Decimal Dot-to-Dot

Improve your understanding of decimals while solving a dot-to-dot picture puzzle.

Procedure

1. Use a copy machine to copy the dot-to-dot puzzle.

2. Starting at 0.0, connect the dots in order from the smallest decimal to the largest.

0.0

● 0.0004

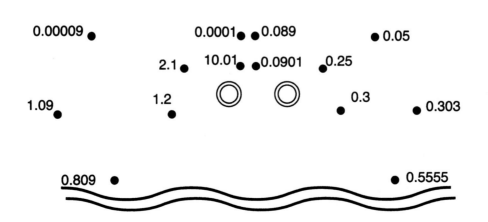

0.00009 ●

0.0001● ●0.089

● 0.05

2.1● 10.01● ●0.0901 ●0.25

1.09●

1.2
●

0.3
●

● 0.303

0.809 ●

● 0.5555

Tips and Tricks

Compare the decimals first by the numbers in the tenths place, then by the numbers in the hundredths place, then by the numbers in the thousandths place.

BRAIN Stretcher

Create your own decimal dot-to-dot. Make a list of decimals. Place them in order from the smallest to the largest. Think of a picture and arrange a series of dots on a piece of paper to make that picture when they are connected. Label the dots with the decimals so that they can be connected in the correct order.

Dynamite Decimal Reduction

To change a decimal to a fraction, use the numerals of the decimal to form the numerator (number above the fraction bar) of the fraction. The denominator (the number below the fraction bar) of the fraction is always a multiple of ten, such as 10, 100, 1000, and so on. You can tell which multiple of ten by looking at the place value of the numeral farthest to the right in the decimal. (Here's another way to find the denominator: it should contain the same number of zeros as there are numerals to the right of the decimal.) Once the decimal is converted to a fraction, reduce it to the lowest common denominator. (See the Tips and Tricks box for a reminder about how to reduce fractions.)

EXAMPLE

To change 0.4 to a fraction, place 4 in the numerator. Since 0.4 has the 4 in the tenths place, use 10 for the denominator. Write it as the fraction $4/10$. Reduce $4/10$ to $2/5$.

To change 0.55 to a fraction, place 55 in the numerator. Since 0.55 means fifty-five hundredths, the denominator is 100. Write it as the fraction $55/100$. Reduce $55/100$ to $11/20$.

Play this game with some friends to practice converting decimals to fractions and reducing them.

Game Preparation

1. Remove all the tens and face cards (kings, queens, and jacks) from a deck of playing cards.

2. Separate the remaining red cards from the remaining black cards. (Save the black cards for the Brain Stretcher section.)

Game Rules

1. Shuffle the red cards and place them facedown in the center of the table.

2. Player 1 turns over the top card and places it face up in the center of the table. The red card represents a decimal fraction in tenths. For example, the three of hearts or the three of diamonds represents 0.3 (three-tenths). The six of hearts or the six of diamonds represents 0.6 (six-tenths).

3. Both players change the decimal to a fraction and reduce it to the smallest fraction possible. The first player to shout out the smallest correct fraction wins the card. For example, if the 5 of diamonds is turned over, the first player to shout out "One-half!" wins the card. If the ace of hearts is turned over, the first player to shout out "One-tenth!" wins the card. Remember that aces are the same as ones.

4. The player who gets the most cards wins the game.

SUPER REDUCING DECIMALS

Play the game the same way except this time use the black cards to represent the hundredths place in each decimal fraction. Pick up both a black card and a red card from the top of each pile. The number on the red card becomes the number in the tenths place and the number on the black card becomes the number in the hundredths place. For example, the seven of hearts and the eight of spades would be 0.78. The six of hearts and the ace of clubs would be 0.61.

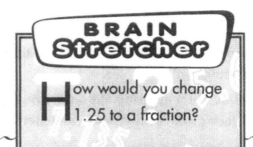

BRAIN Stretcher

How would you change 1.25 to a fraction?

Tips and Tricks

To reduce a fraction to lowest terms, divide the numerator and denominator by the same number. (If you cannot find a number that will divide evenly into both the numerator and denominator, the fraction is in lowest terms.)

Examples:

1. Reduce $^{25}/_{30}$.

Divide 25 and 30 by 5.

$^{25}/_{30} = ^{5}/_{6}$

5 and 6 cannot be divided by the same number, so $^{5}/_{6}$ is in lowest terms.

2. Reduce $^{3}/_{11}$.

3 and 11 cannot be divided by the same number, therefore $^{3}/_{11}$ is in lowest terms.

3. Reduce $^{6}/_{12}$.

Divide 6 and 12 by 2.

$^{3}/_{6}$ is still not in lowest terms. Divide 3 and 6 by 3.

$^{3}/_{6} = ^{1}/_{2}$

$^{1}/_{2}$ is in lowest terms.

Batting It In

To change a fraction to a decimal, divide the numerator by the denominator. Practice changing fractions to decimals while you study the statistics of your favorite baseball team.

MATERIALS

computer with
Internet access or
a newspaper with
sports statistics
pencil
paper
calculator

Procedure

1. Log on to the Internet. Go to the website www.mlb.com. If you don't have a computer with Internet access, look in the sports section of your local newspaper for the batting statistics of your favorite baseball team and skip to step 4.

2. At MLB, click on stats at the top of the page and pick your favorite baseball team. Click on batting statistics. Get the batting statistics for the entire season. You will find a list of the players on the team and their individual statistics.

3. Copy the chart shown here onto your sheet of paper.

Players and Positions	AB	H	AVG	HR	HR AVG

4. Write the names of the players on your team and their positions in the chart.

5. Copy the numbers from the AB column (which stands for at bats) onto your chart. This is the number of times the player was at bat.

6. Copy the numbers from the H column (which stands for hits) onto your chart. This is the number of times the player got a hit. A hit is a single, double, triple, or home run.

7. AVG stands for the player's batting average. Find each player's batting average by dividing the number of hits by the number of at bats. Use the calculator for help. Enter the averages in the chart.

$$AVG = {}^{H}\!/_{AB}$$

Does your answer match the answer found on the Internet or in the newspaper under AVG?

8. Copy the numbers from the HR column (which stands for home runs) onto your chart. This is the number of home runs each player got.

9. Now compute each player's HR AVG (home run average) by dividing the number of home runs (HR) by the number of at bats (AB). Use the calculator for help. Enter the results in the chart.

$$HR\ AVG = {}^{HR}\!/\!_{AB}$$

10. Who has the highest average on the team? Who has the highest HR average on the team? What positions do the players with the highest averages play?

BRAIN Stretcher

Use the website to look up league leaders (players with the highest batting average or the most home runs).

Slap Match

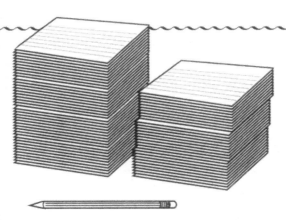

Practice matching common fractions to their decimal equivalents.

Game Preparation

Write one of the following fractions or decimals on each index card:

$1/10$	0.1	$3/5$	0.6	$12/20$	0.6
$2/10$	0.2	$4/5$	0.8	$15/20$	0.75
$3/10$	0.3	$5/5$	1	$16/20$	0.8
$4/10$	0.4	$1/4$	0.25	$1/8$	0.125
$5/10$	0.5	$2/4$	0.5	$2/8$	0.25
$6/10$	0.6	$3/4$	0.75	$3/8$	0.375
$7/10$	0.7	$4/4$	1	$4/8$	0.5
$8/10$	0.8	$1/20$	.05	$5/8$	0.625
$9/10$	0.9	$3/20$	0.15	$6/8$	0.75
$10/10$	1	$4/20$	0.2	$7/8$	0.875
$1/5$	0.2	$5/20$	0.25	$8/8$	1
$2/5$	0.4	$10/20$	0.5		

Game Rules

1. Shuffle the index cards and deal each player half the cards. Each player should place his or her cards facedown in front of himself or herself.

2. Player 1 turns over his or her top card and places it in the center of the table.

3. Player 2 turns over his or her top card and places it on top of player 1's card. Players take turns adding cards face up to the center of the stack.

4. When two consecutive cards have the same value, players slap the stack of cards. The first player to slap the stack of cards wins the entire stack. Remember the idea is to match up fractions and decimals that have the same values.

5. If a player slaps the stack of cards when the two top cards do not have the same value, the other player wins the stack of cards.

6. Continue until one player wins all the cards.

Tips and Tricks

If you memorize the common fraction and decimal pairs used in this game, you'll not only become a champion at Slap Match, you'll always be able to change these fractions to their decimals and back again, just like that!

Decimals Forever

A repeating decimal is a decimal in which the same numeral or series of numerals repeats forever. Here's a game that will help you learn to recognize repeating decimals.

MATERIALS

2 players
deck of playing cards
2 sheets of paper
2 pencils
die

Game Preparation

1. Remove all of the face cards (kings, queens, and jacks) from a deck of playing cards.

2. Give each person a piece of paper and a pencil.

Game Rules

1. Shuffle the cards and place them facedown in the center of the table.

2. Player 1 rolls the die. The number rolled is the numerator of the fraction.

3. Payer 2 turns over the top card. The number on the card is the denominator of the fraction.

4. Both players convert the fraction to a decimal by dividing the numerator by the denominator. Players may use paper and pencil to do their calculating.

5. If the decimal is a repeating decimal, players yell "Repeating!" and tap the card. The first player to tap the card wins the top card and all the cards under it.

6. Player 2 turns over the next card and both players use this as the next denominator with the same numerator. Repeat steps 4 and 5.

7. Continue going through the stack of cards one by one. When all the cards are gone, the player with the most cards wins the round.

8. Player 2 rolls the die to find a new numerator. Player 1 shuffles the cards and places them facedown in the center of the table. Player 1 turns over the top card and players start the next round.

9. The first player to win three rounds wins the game.

Tips and Tricks

One-third is a fraction that converts to a repeating decimal. Change ⅓ to a decimal by dividing 1 by 3.

$$\begin{array}{r} .3333 \\ 3\overline{)1.000} \end{array}$$

To indicate a repeating decimal, put a bar over the number or numbers that repeat like this: $⅓ = .\overline{3}$

Change ⅑ to a decimal.

$$\begin{array}{r} .11111 \\ 9\overline{)1.00000} \end{array}$$

$$⅑ = .\overline{1}$$

Sometimes a repeating decimal includes a series of repeat numerals.

$$1/11 = 0.09090909 \ldots \text{ or } .\overline{09}$$

$$1/7 = 0.142857142857 \ldots \text{ or } 0.\overline{142857}$$

ADDING AND SUBTRACTING DECIMALS

Now that you know decimal basics, it is time to learn how to add and subtract decimals. You'll learn how to add and subtract decimal numbers and decimal numbers that are greater than one. And, of course, you'll learn how to subtract a decimal from a whole number, which is always a tricky feat. Along the way, you'll figure out all the combinations of change that make a dollar, go on a shopping spree, compare the costs of sending a package, and play lots of fun games.

Dozens of Dollars

To add decimals together, you first match up the decimal points, then add the two numbers as you would add any two numbers. Remember to start adding on the right and carry to the left. In this activity you will convert coins to their decimal equivalents and find different ways to add these decimals so that they make one dollar.

MATERIALS

2 half-dollars
4 quarters
10 dimes
20 nickels
pencil
paper
calculator

Game Preparation

Every coin in the American monetary system actually represents part of one whole dollar. For example, 25 cents is the same as 0.25 of a dollar. Dollars are written as whole numbers and the coins are written as decimals. Here is how to write the decimal equivalent of each coin.

One half-dollar = 0.50

One quarter = 0.25

One dime = 0.10

One nickel = 0.05

One penny = 0.01

To add the values of two coins together, you can just add their decimal values. For example, to add two quarters, just add 0.25 and 0.25. Keep the decimal point in the same place and be sure to include it in your answer.

$$
\begin{array}{r}
0.25 \\
+0.25 \\
\hline
0.50
\end{array}
$$

Twenty-five cents plus twenty-five cents equals fifty cents.

To add a quarter, a nickel, and a dime, convert them to their decimal values, line up the decimal points, and add the numbers.

$$
\begin{array}{r}
0.25 \\
0.05 \\
+0.10 \\
\hline
0.40
\end{array}
$$

If you have a quarter, a nickel, and a dime, you have forty cents.
How much are two quarters, three dimes, and four nickels worth?
Add the decimal values of the coins to find out.

$$
\begin{array}{r}
0.25 \\
0.25 \\
0.10 \\
0.10 \\
0.10 \\
0.05 \\
0.05 \\
0.05 \\
+0.05 \\
\hline
1.00
\end{array}
$$

If you have two quarters, three dimes, and four nickels, you have one dollar! Note that the 1 was carried over to the ones place.

Game Rules

1. There are many different ways you can make $1 using nickels, dimes, quarters, and half-dollars. Think of as many combinations as you can and write them down. Check your addition by adding the values of the coins on a calculator.

2. Answer the following questions. Try to answer them first without a calculator, then check your math.

- You can make a dollar with just nickels. How many nickels do you need?

- You can also make a dollar with just dimes. How many dimes does it take?

- What if you made a dollar using only quarters? How many quarters do you need?

- There is only one way to make a dollar using only quarters and dimes. Can you figure out what it is?

- There are nine different ways to make a dollar using both nickels and dimes. Can you figure them all out?

- There are eleven ways to make a dollar when one of the coins is a half-dollar. What are they?

- There are only two different ways to make a dollar using at least one of each coin. What are they?

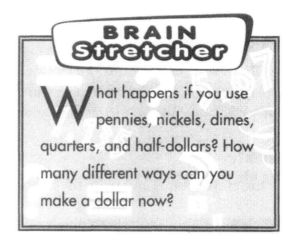

BRAIN Stretcher

What happens if you use pennies, nickels, dimes, quarters, and half-dollars? How many different ways can you make a dollar now?

Dazzling Decimal Addition

To add decimals and whole numbers, put the decimals
in a vertical column one on top of the other. Be sure
to line up the decimal points. In the answer, place the decimal
point directly underneath the other decimal
points. Play this game to practice adding
decimals and whole numbers.

MATERIALS

2 or more players

deck of playing
cards

4 pennies

pencils

paper

Game Preparation

1. Remove all the 10s and face cards (kings, queens, and jacks) from the
deck of playing cards. Remember that aces are the same as ones.

2. Give each player two pennies.

Game Rules

1. Shuffle the playing cards and place them facedown in the center of the
table.

2. Deal each player four cards. Each player places his or her cards facedown
in two rows with two cards in each row. Each player places a penny to
the right of each set of two cards. The pennies represent the decimal
points.

3. One player says "Go" and both players turn over their cards. Players move all red cards to the right of the decimal point. All black cards stay to the left of the decimal point.

4. Both players add their decimal numbers and write their answers on a sheet of paper.

5. The first player to add his or her two numbers together correctly wins the round.

6. The used cards are discarded and the dealer deals each player six new cards. Each player places his or her cards facedown in two rows of three cards each. Each player places a decimal point (penny) to the right of each set of three cards.

7. One player says "Go" and both players turn over their cards. Players move all red cards to the right of the decimal point. All black cards stay to the left of the decimal point.

8. Both players add their decimal numbers and write their answers on a sheet of paper.

9. The first player to add his or her two numbers together correctly wins the round.

10. The used cards are discarded and the dealer deals each player eight new cards. Each player places his or her cards facedown in two rows of four cards each. Each player places a penny to the right of each set of four cards.

11. One player says "Go" and both players turn over their cards. Players move all red cards to the right of the decimal point. All black cards stay to the left of the decimal point.

12. Both players add their decimal numbers and write their answers on a sheet of paper.

13. The first player to add his or her two numbers together correctly wins the round.

14. The player who wins two out of three rounds wins the game.

Count Down

Subtracting decimals is easy. To subtract one decimal from another decimal, just line up the decimal points and subtract as you would any two numbers. Start at the right and move to the left. In the answer, place the decimal point right under the other decimal points. If one decimal is shorter than the other, put zeros at the end to make both numbers the same length.

MATERIALS

2 players
4 dice
pencil
paper

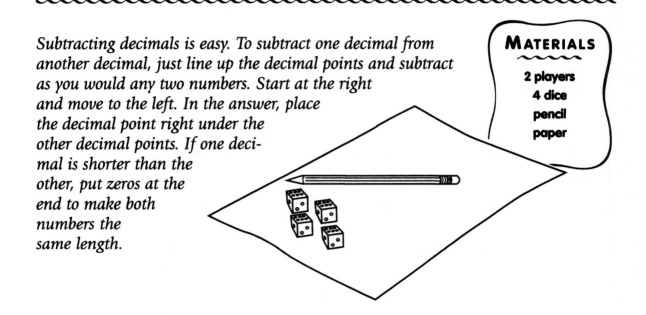

EXAMPLE

$7.50
−2.25
$5.25

0.5 − 0.32 =

0.50
−0.32
0.18

Play this game with a friend to practice subtracting one decimal from another decimal.

Game Rules

1. Players roll two dice to see who goes first.

2. Both players write 0.99 on a sheet of paper.

3. Player 1 rolls two dice and uses that number to create a decimal (using one of the numbers to represent tenths and one to represent hundredths). Player 1 subtracts the number rolled from 0.99. *Example:* If a player rolls a 3 and 2, the decimal created could be 0.32 or 0.23. Player 1 chooses 0.23 and subtracts it from 0.99. The result is 0.76.

4. Player 2 rolls two dice, creates a decimal, and subtracts the result from 0.99.

5. Player 1 rolls two dice and subtracts the rolled decimal from the former difference. *Example:* If player 1 rolls a 6 and a 6, the created decimal 0.66 is subtracted from 0.76. The result is 0.10.

6. Player 2 rolls the dice and the play continues until the number rolled is larger than the number left. In that case, that player loses the round.

7. In round 2, both players start by writing 0.999 on a sheet of paper and each player rolls three dice.

8. In round 3, both players start by writing 0.9999 on a sheet of paper and each player rolls four dice.

9. The player who wins two out of three rounds wins the game.

Overnight Delivery

Practice subtracting one decimal from another as you compare the costs of sending a package by different shipping services.

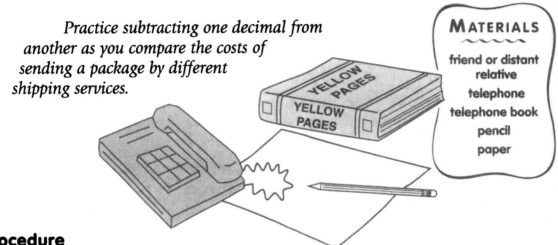

Procedure

1. Find the address of a friend or relative who lives far away from you and write it down on a piece of paper.

2. Look up the following phone numbers in your phone book: U.S. Post Office, Federal Express, United Parcel Service.

3. Call each of these shipping services and ask how much it would cost to send a letter for next-day delivery from your town to your friend's or relative's house. You must be able to tell the delivery service the address and zip code to find the correct price.

4. Find the answers to these questions:

Which is the most expensive shipping service?

Which is the least expensive shipping service?

Subtract the least expensive service from the most expensive service. What is the difference in price?

Shopping Spree

To subtract decimals
and whole numbers,
just place a decimal point
after the whole number and add
enough zeros so that both
numbers have the same
number of places after the
decimal point.

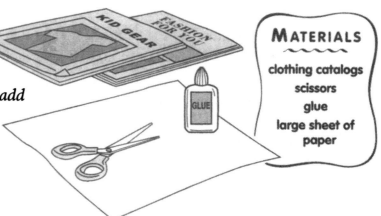

MATERIALS

clothing catalogs
scissors
glue
large sheet of
paper

EXAMPLE

$$\$10 - \$2.99 =$$

$$
\begin{array}{r}
\$10.00 \\
-\ \$2.99 \\
\hline
\$7.01
\end{array}
$$

Practice subtracting decimals and whole numbers as you pretend
to shop for clothes.

Procedure

1. Pretend your parents gave you $100 for a clothing allowance and you
   are going to go on a shopping spree. And let's imagine you live in
   Delaware, where there is no tax on clothing, and the catalogs you are
   using are offering free shipping.

2. Cut pictures of clothing that you might like to buy out of the catalogs.

3. From the cut-out pictures, pick your first item. Can you afford it? If you can afford it, subtract the price from your $100 clothing allowance. Remember to add zeros if you need them so that your $100 clothing allowance looks like this: $100.00.

4. Now pick something else. If you can afford it with the money you have left, subtract the price from that amount.

5. Continue selecting clothing and subtracting the price from the money you have left until the amount of money you have left is too small to buy anything else. How far does your $100 go? Glue the pictures of what you bought for $100 on the large sheet of paper.

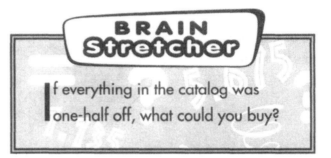

BRAIN Stretcher

If everything in the catalog was one-half off, what could you buy?

Zeros Exchange

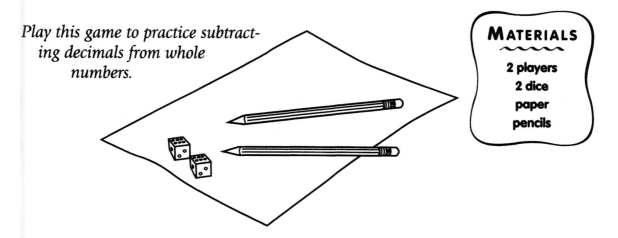

Play this game to practice subtracting decimals from whole numbers.

Game Rules

1. Each player rolls a single die. The number on the die is the number the player will use to construct a subtraction problem. The number rolled is also the number of zeros the players will use in constructing a subtraction problem.

2. Each player uses the number he or she rolled to write one problem that includes a whole number minus a decimal.

EXAMPLES

If a player rolls a 1, the player must use only the numeral 1 and one zero. Possible problems are

$$1 - 0.01$$
$$10 - 0.1$$

If a player rolls a 2, the player must use only the numeral 2 and two zeros. Possible problems are

$$2 - 0.002$$
$$2 - 0.020$$
$$20 - 0.02$$
$$20 - 0.20$$
$$200 - 0.2$$

3. Players exchange problems and solve them. A point is given to the first person to solve the problem he or she was given.

4. Players each roll a single die again, and design and solve new problems.

5. The first player to earn 10 points wins the game.

~~~~ IV ~~~~

MULTIPLYING AND DIVIDING DECIMALS

Now that you know how to add and subtract decimals, it's time to learn how to multiply decimals with decimals and decimals with whole numbers, and to divide a decimal by a decimal and a decimal by a whole number. There are lots of different types of multiplication and division problems, but once you get the hang of doing them, you'll see that the principles are the same for each problem.

In this section, as you learn how to work with decimals, you'll also figure out how much fast-food prices have increased since the 1960s, you'll learn how to convert money from one currency to another, and you'll even decipher a coded message.

Multiplication War

*When you multiply two decimals, multiply the two numbers
as if they were whole numbers. Then count the number of
numerals to the right of the decimal point in both numbers
and add them together. Starting at the
right of the answer, count to the
left this number of places. Place a
decimal point there.*

EXAMPLE

What is 0.004×0.12? Multiply as if the numerals were whole numbers:
$4 \times 12 = 48$. Count the numerals to the right of the decimal points in the
original problem. There are five. Count five spaces to the left in the product of your multiplication problem and put the decimal point there. Add
zeros if you run out of places. The answer is 0.00048.

Play this fast-paced card game to practice multiplying two decimals.

Game Preparation

Remove the face cards (kings, queens, and jacks) and 10s from a deck of
playing cards. There should be 36 cards left. Remember that aces are the
same as ones.

Game Rules

1. Deal each player 18 cards. Both players place their cards facedown in a
    stack in front of them.

2. Each player turns his or her top card over at the same time and both players multiply the values of these two cards. The black cards represent tenths and the red cards represent hundredths.

Example. One player draws the six of spades. Since spades are black, the six goes in the tenths place: 0.6. The other player draws the six of diamonds. Since diamonds are red, the six goes in the hundredths place: 0.06. Both players multiply 0.6 times 0.06 as fast as they can. The first player to shout out the correct answer (0.036) wins both cards.

3. If both players shout out the correct answer at exactly the same time, it's a multiplication war. Both players simultaneously place three new cards facedown and a fourth new card face up in front of them. The first player to shout out the correct product of the two face-up cards wins all 10 cards!

4. The game continues until one player wins all the cards.

Tips and Tricks

1. When you multiply a tenth by a tenth, the answer is always in the hundredths.

Example: 0.1 × 0.5 = 0.05 (five-hundredths)
Example: 0.3 × 0.7 = 0.21 (twenty-one hundredths)

2. When you multiply a hundredth by a hundredth, the answer is always in the ten-thousandths.

Example: 0.03 × 0.06 = 0.0018 (eighteen ten-thousandths)
Example: 0.01 × 0.01 = 0.0001 (one ten-thousandth)

3. When you multiply a tenth by a hundredth, the answer is always in the thousandths.   Example: 0.4 × 0.01 = 0.004 (four-thousandths)

Inflation

To multiply a decimal by a whole number, first multiply the two numbers as if they were both whole numbers. Next count the number of places to the right of the decimal point in the decimal number. Starting at the right of the answer, count to the left the same number of spaces you counted in the decimal number. Place the decimal point there.

EXAMPLE

What is 0.6 × 700? First multiply: 6 × 700 = 4200. Move the decimal point in the answer one space to the left. The answer becomes 420.0 or 420.

Practice multiplying decimals by whole numbers as you compare the prices of fast food now to what they were in the 1960s.

Procedure

1. Copy the chart below on a piece of paper.

2. In 1964, a fast-food hamburger cost 15 cents, an order of fries was 15 cents, a small drink was 10 cents, and a shake was 20 cents. Enter these prices in your chart.

3. Visit a local fast-food restaurant and look up the prices of a hamburger, small fries, a small drink, and a shake. (Don't count value meals.) Enter these prices in the chart.

Item	1964 Prices	Today's Prices	Your Family's Order	Total Cost at 1964 Prices	Total Cost at Today's Prices
Hamburger					
French Fries					
Small Drink					
Shake					
Total					

4. Now pretend you are going to order lunch for your family. Ask everyone what he or she would want from the food on your list. Write the number of orders for each item on your chart.

5. Compute how much your family's lunch would cost today and how much it would have cost in 1964 by multiplying the price of each item by the number of each item ordered and adding all the totals.

   Example: An order of fries costs $1.25 today. Two people ordered fries. Multiply: $1.25 × 2. First make the decimal a whole number and multiply: 125 × 2 = 250. Next count the number of spaces to the right of the decimal point in the decimal number. There are two spaces to the right of the decimal point in the number 1.25. Move the decimal point two spaces to the left in the answer to get $2.50. The total order of fries is $2.50. Add this to the total orders of other foods to get the cost of the total meal.

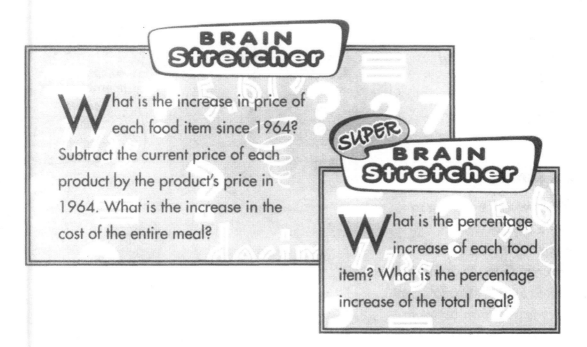

BRAIN Stretcher

What is the increase in price of each food item since 1964? Subtract the current price of each product by the product's price in 1964. What is the increase in the cost of the entire meal?

SUPER BRAIN Stretcher

What is the percentage increase of each food item? What is the percentage increase of the total meal?

Currency Exchange

*Learn how to multiply
whole numbers and
decimals as
you convert money from
different countries.*

MATERIALS

computer with
Internet access
paper
pencil
calculator

Procedure

1. Imagine you are going to
take a trip to Mexico.
Mexico uses a different
currency than we do in the
United States. Mexico's currency is based on the peso.

2. Log on to the Internet and go to the website
www.xe.com. You will find a currency converter there that can calculate
what your dollars are worth in another currency. What is the exchange
rate for dollars to Mexican pesos?

3. Multiply dollars by the exchange rate to find out how many Mexican
pesos you would get for $1, $10, $20, and $100. Check your calculations
using the currency converter.

4. Compute the number of pesos you would need to buy the following
items in Mexico (assuming they were the same price). Use a calculator to
help you with the calculations.

Items	Price in Dollars	Exchange Rate	Price in Pesos
Cola Drink	$1		
Hotel Room	$135/night		
Film	$4		
Gum	$.50		
Rental Car	$300/week		
Dinner at Hotel	$18		

Graph the exchange rate between the U.S. dollar and the Japanese yen over a one-month period. What do you notice?

Exchange rates change on a daily basis. Log back on to www.xe.com one week later and find the new exchange rate for the Mexican peso. Compute the percentage increase or decrease since you last checked the rate.

To find the percent change, subtract the old exchange rate from the new exchange rate. Divide this difference by the original rate and multiply by 100.

Example: The Mexican peso was trading at 9 pesos to the dollar. It is currently trading at 10 pesos to the dollar. Subtract the old rate from the new rate: 10 − 9 = 1. Divide this difference (1) by the original exchange rate (9). $\frac{1}{9} = 0.11$. Multiply 0.11 by 100 to find the percentage change. $0.11 \times 100 = 11\%$ change.

Crack the Code!

To divide a decimal by a decimal, change the divisor (the number you are dividing by) to a whole number by moving the decimal point to the right. Next, move the decimal point in the dividend (the number you are dividing) the same number of places to the right. Divide as you normally would.

MATERIALS

pencil
paper

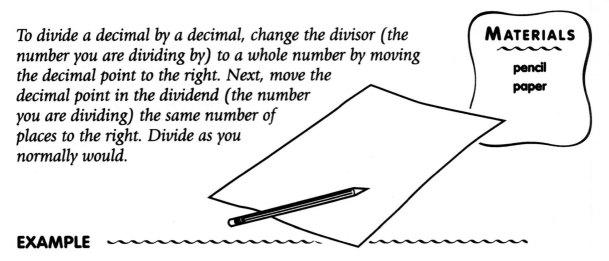

EXAMPLE

What is 0.27 ÷ 0.003?

Move the decimal point in both numbers three spaces to the right to change the problem to 270 ÷ 3.

The answer is 90.

What is 10 ÷ 0.02?

Change the problem to 1,000 divided by 2.

The answer is 500.

Now learn to read secret messages as you practice dividing a decimal by a decimal.

Procedure

1. Solve the division problems listed below.

2. Match each answer to the correct letter according to the chart. Put the letters together to read the secret message.

A	C	E	G	I	M	S
1000	100	10	1	.1	.01	.001

		Number	Letter
1.	0.0002 ÷ by 0.02	_____	_____
2.	0.8 ÷ by 0.0008	_____	_____
3.	0.648 ÷ 0.648	_____	_____
4.	0.017 ÷ 0.17	_____	_____
5.	0.45 ÷ 0.0045	_____	_____
6.	0.005 ÷ 0.5	_____	_____
7.	0.07 ÷ 0.007	_____	_____
8.	0.0002 ÷ 0.2	_____	_____
9.	0.0006 ÷ 0.6	_____	_____
10.	0.50 ÷ 0.0005	_____	_____
11.	0.004 ÷ 0.004	_____	_____
12.	0.13 ÷ 0.013	_____	_____

Now fill in the letters to read the secret message:

___ ___ ___ ___ ___ ___ ___ ___ ___ ___ ___ ___
 1   2   3   4   5   6   7   8   9   10   11   12

53

Create your own coded message. Make a code and create decimal division problems that reveal the answer. See if your friends can read your secret message.

Tips and Tricks

To multiply a number by 10, move the decimal point one space to the right.

To multiply a number by 100, move the decimal point two spaces to the right.

To divide a number by 10, move the decimal point one space to the left.

To divide a number by 100, move the decimal point two spaces to the left.

15-Second Division

To divide a whole number by a decimal, you have to change both the dividend and the divisor. First change the divisor to a whole number by moving the decimal point to the right the number of spaces necessary to make the divisor a whole number.
Count the number of spaces you moved the decimal point. Now add the same number of zeros to the end of the dividend and divide.

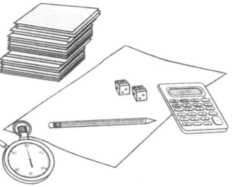

MATERIALS

2 players
pencil
22 index cards
2 dice
paper
stopwatch or clock with second hand
calculator

EXAMPLE

What is 27 ÷ 0.003? In the divisor (0.003), move the decimal point three spaces to the right to get the whole number 3. Add three zeros to the end of the dividend (27,000). Now divide. So 27 divided by 0.003 is 9,000.

$$\begin{array}{r} 9{,}000 \\ 3\overline{)27{,}000} \end{array}$$

To divide a decimal by a whole number, just divide. Put a decimal in the quotient at a spot directly above the decimal in the dividend. Add zeros as place holders if necessary.

$$0.0032 \div 4 =$$

$$\begin{array}{r} .0008 \\ 4\overline{).0032} \end{array}$$

$$0.0032 \div 4 = 0.0008$$

Here is a fun way to practice division with decimals and whole numbers.

Game Preparation

1. Write one of the following decimal numbers on each of the index cards:

0.5	0.25	0.0002
0.05	0.025	0.3
0.005	0.0025	0.04
0.0005	0.000025	0.006
0.1	0.2	0.0007
0.01	0.02	0.00008
0.001	0.002	0.000009
0.00001		

2. Copy the score sheet on page 57.

Game Rules

1. Shuffle the index cards and place them facedown in the center of the table.

2. Player 1 turns over the top card and places it face up on the table. Player 1 rolls the dice.

3. The number on the index card and the number rolled are used to create two different division problems: (1) the number on the index card divided by the number rolled and (2) the number rolled divided by the number on the index card. For example, if the index card reads 0.04 and the number rolled on the dice is 8, the two problems are 0.04 ÷ 8 and 8 ÷ 0.04.

4. Player 1 uses paper and pencil to solve both division problems. In round 1, player 1 has 60 seconds to solve both problems. Player 2 keeps track of the time and checks the answers using the calculator. Player 1 is awarded one point for each problem solved correctly and one bonus point if both problems are solved correctly. The score is recorded on the score sheet.

5. Player 2 turns over the next card and rolls the dice. Player 2 has 60 seconds to solve both problems created by these two numbers. Player 1 keeps track of the time and checks player 2's answers. This score is recorded on the score sheet.

6. The game continues for three more rounds. During each round, players are given less time to solve the problems. In the second round players have 45 seconds, in the third round players have 30 seconds, and in the fourth they have 15 seconds.

7. The player with the most points after four rounds wins the game.

SCORE SHEET

	Player 1	Player 2
Round 1 Score (60 seconds)		
Round 2 Score (45 seconds)		
Round 3 Score (30 seconds)		
Round 4 Score (15 seconds)		
Total Score		

Buckets of Change

Here is another way to practice dividing a decimal by a whole number.

MATERIALS

2 players
bowl of change
pencil
paper
die
6 cups

Game Rules

1. Player 1 takes a handful of change from the bowl, counts the change, and writes the total on a sheet of paper.

2. Player 1 rolls the die and places as many cups as the number rolled on the table.

3. Player 1 must divide the change between the selected cups. If necessary, player 1 can use the bowl of change to exchange coins for coins of smaller denominations. For example, imagine player 1 takes a handful of change adding up to $1.71. He or she then rolls a 3 on the die. He or she needs to figure out how to divide $1.71 into three cups evenly. Player 1 needs to put coins adding up to 57 cents in each cup.

4. When player 1 is done, he or she counts the change in one of the cups. Player 2 checks player 1's work by dividing the total amount of the change by the number rolled. If player 1 is correct, this is his or her score. If player 1 is incorrect, he or she gets no points.

5. Now player 2 takes player 1's place and repeats the process. Player 1 checks player 2's work.

6. The first player to win 300 points wins the game.

Watch the Trends

Look for patterns in dividing whole numbers by decimals.

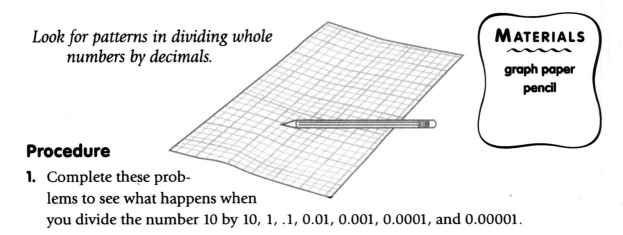

Procedure

1. Complete these problems to see what happens when you divide the number 10 by 10, 1, .1, 0.01, 0.001, 0.0001, and 0.00001.

$$10 \div 10$$

$$10 \div 1$$

$$10 \div 0.1$$

$$10 \div 0.01$$

$$10 \div 0.001$$

$$10 \div 0.0001$$

$$10 \div 0.00001$$

What did you notice about your answers? In all seven problems, the dividend is the same: 10. In each consecutive problem, the divisor decreases from 10 to 1 to 0.1 to 0.01 to 0.001 to 0.0001 to 0.00001. Notice that as the divisor decreases by a factor of 10, the quotient increases by a factor of 10 from 1 to 10 to 100 to 1,000 to 10,000 to 100,000 to 1,000,000.

2. Use the graph paper to make a graph showing the divisors and quotients of each problem. What do you notice?

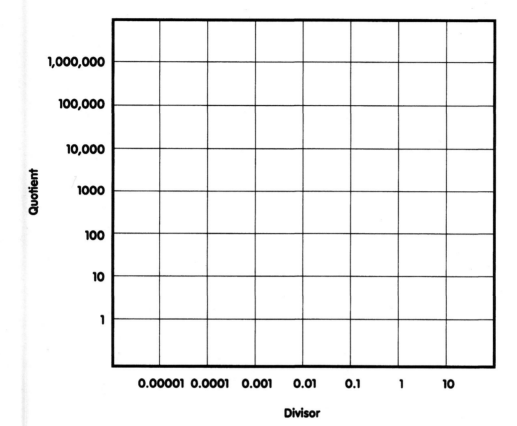

3. Solve and graph the following problems. What do you notice?

$2 \div 5 =$

$2 \div 0.5 =$

$2 \div 0.05 =$

$2 \div 0.005 =$

$2 \div 0.0005 =$

$2 \div 0.00005 =$

V

THE FACTS ON PERCENTS

The word *percent* means one part in a hundred, or divided by 100, and in this section you'll learn all about percents. You'll learn what percents are, how to estimate a percent, and how to change percents to decimals and fractions and back again. You'll also learn how to solve four types of percent problems: (1) finding an unknown percentage, (2) taking the percentage of a number, (3) finding the missing base, and (4) calculating the percentage of an increase or decrease.

While you're learning all about percents, you'll also have fun creating optical illusions, designing a conversion wheel that helps convert percents to fractions and decimals, figuring out how much juice is really in a "juice drink," and discovering what percentage of colored candy in a bag of colored candy is red.

23

Percent Grids

What exactly is a percentage? Try this activity to draw a picture of what percents look like.

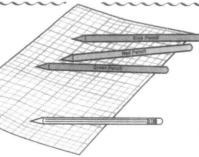

MATERIALS

pencil
graph paper
colored pencils

Procedure

1. On a piece of graph paper, draw six squares ten boxes long and ten boxes wide. Each square of the large square contains 100 small squares. Each of these small squares is 1 percent of the large square.

2. In the first large square, shade 1 small square. Write 1% in the shaded area. This small square is 1% of the total area of the large square ($^1/_{100}$).

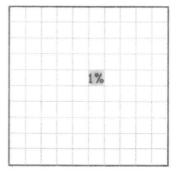

3. In the second large square, shade 10 small squares in a row. Write 10% in the shaded area. This group of squares is 10% of the total area of the large square ($^{10}/_{100}$, which reduces to $^1/_{10}$).

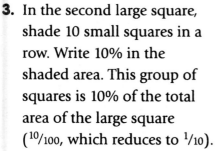

4. In the third large square, shade 25 of the small squares. Write 25% in the shaded area. This area is 25% of the total area of the large square ($^{25}/_{100}$, which reduces to $^1/_4$).

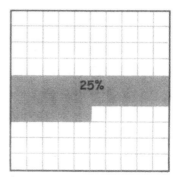

5. In the fourth large square, shade 50 of the small squares. Write 50% in the shaded area. This area is 50% of the total of the large square ($^{50}/_{100}$, which reduces to $^{1}/_{2}$).

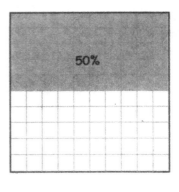

6. In the fifth large square, shade 75 of the small squares. Write 75% in the shaded area. This area is 75% of the total area of the large square ($^{75}/_{100}$, which reduces to $^{3}/_{4}$).

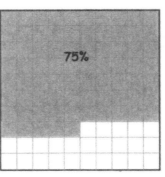

7. In the last square, shade all but one of the small squares. Write 99% in the shaded area. This area is 99% of the total area of the large square ($^{99}/_{100}$).

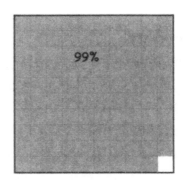

BRAIN Stretcher

1. On a second sheet of graph paper, draw a set of five 10-by-10 squares.

2. Shade 25 small squares in each of these large squares, but shade a *different* 25 small squares in each large square. Try to make the patterns look very different. Use the colored pencils to shade these drawings and make different patterns.

3. Ask a friend which square has more shaded squares. Is he or she fooled?

Guessing Game

You can estimate percentages by looking at the numerator and denominator of a fraction. If the numerator is greater than half of the denominator, the fraction is greater than 50%. If it is less, it is less than 50%.

To change a fraction to a percent, first change the fraction to a decimal by dividing the numerator by the denominator. Next multiply the answer by 100.

MATERIALS

2 players
pencil
index cards
2 dice

EXAMPLE

Change $\frac{1}{4}$ to a percent. First change $\frac{1}{4}$ to a decimal: $\frac{1}{4} = 0.25$. Multiply the answer by 100: $100 \times 0.25 = 25\%$

Practice estimating percentages and changing fractions to percents.

Game Preparation

Write each of the following food items on an index card:

French fries (100 to a pack)

Soft drinks (6 to a pack)

Cupcakes (2 to a pack)

Donuts (12 to a pack)

Juice boxes (10 to a pack)

Colored candy (50 to a pack)

Potato chips (100 to a bag)

Eggs (12 to a dozen)

Ice-cream sandwiches (6 to a box)

Pizza (8 slices to a pie)

Chocolate cake (8 slices to a cake)

Candy (2 pieces to a pack)

Game Rules

1. Deal each player five cards. A player may look at his or her own cards but should not show them to the other player.

2. One player rolls the die. The number on the die indicates how many of an item a player can choose. For example, if a 2 is rolled, a player may choose 2 eggs, 2 cupcakes, 2 potato chips, and so on.

3. Once the number is rolled, each player selects one card from his or her hand of five and places it on the table. Each player should try to estimate which item when combined with that number will create the highest percentage. The player with the highest percentage wins both cards.

   For example, if a 3 is rolled and player 1 selects the egg card, 3 out of 12 eggs is $^3/_{12}$, or 25%. If player 2 selects the ice-cream sandwiches, 3 out of 6 ice-cream sandwiches is $^3/_6$, or 50%, so player 2 wins both cards. (*Note:* No card is worth more

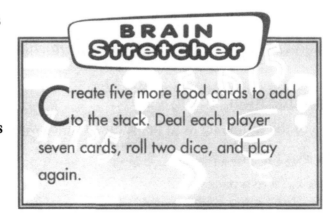

BRAIN Stretcher

Create five more food cards to add to the stack. Deal each player seven cards, roll two dice, and play again.

than 100%. For example, if a 3 is rolled and the player picks the cupcake card (2), the score is still 100%.) After each round, figure out the exact percentages to determine the winner.

4. The die is rolled again and players select a second card from their hands.

5. The game is over when all five cards are played. The player who wins the most pairs of cards is the winner.

Scramble

To change a percent to a decimal, all you need to do is move the decimal point two places to the left.

88% becomes .88.

5% becomes .05.

120% becomes 1.2.

To change a decimal to a percent, just move the decimal point two places to the right.

.03 becomes 3%.

.6 becomes 60%.

5 becomes 500%.

Use this game to practice converting between decimals and percents.

Game Preparation

Write one of the following decimals and percents on each index card:

0.001, 0.005, 0.01, 0.05, 0.10, 0.15, 0.2, 0.25, 0.45, 0.5, 0.55, 0.6, 0.75, 0.9, 1, 2, 2.5, 5, 1%, 5%, 10%, .1%, .5%, 1%, 5%, 15%, 20%, 25%, 45%, 55%, 60%, 75%, 90%, 100%, 200%, 250%

Game Rules

1. Shuffle all the index cards and place them facedown on the table.

2. Player 1 turns over the timer. Both players take two cards from the stack of cards and place them face up on the table.

3. Both players have one minute to place their two cards in order from lowest to highest. If the two cards have the same value, players should place them on top of each other. If both players succeed, the game continues. But if either player fails, he or she loses the game.

4. Next both players turn over three cards from the stack of cards and try to put them in order from lowest to highest in one minute. If either player fails, he or she loses the game.

5. Play continues, and in each successive round the number of cards to unscramble and place in order from lowest to highest is increased by one. The winner is the player who can unscramble the longest string of cards. (If you run out of cards, shuffle all the cards and place them back in the stack.)

BRAIN Stretcher

Write each of the following fractions on an index card and add them to the stack of cards to unscramble:

$\frac{1}{4}$, $\frac{1}{10}$, $\frac{1}{5}$, $\frac{1}{8}$, $\frac{1}{3}$, $\frac{2}{5}$, $\frac{3}{4}$, $\frac{4}{5}$, $\frac{7}{10}$, $\frac{1}{2}$, $\frac{3}{5}$, $\frac{3}{10}$

Conversion Wheel

Create a conversion wheel that converts
percents to fractions and decimals.

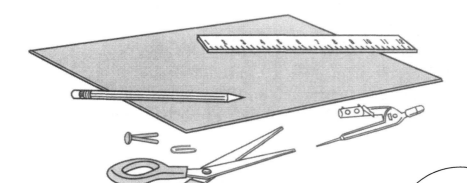

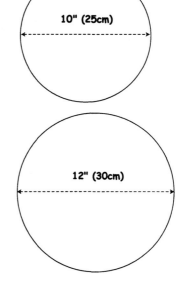

10" (25cm)

12" (30cm)

Procedure

1. Use the compass to draw one circle with a
12-inch (30-cm) diameter (the diameter
is the distance from one side of the circle
to the other) and another circle with a
10-inch (25-cm) diameter on the poster
board.

2. Cut out both circles.

3. In the 10-inch circle, cut out a 1-inch square
window near the circle's outer edge.

4. Write "conversion wheel" on the small circle.

5. Measure the diameter of the small circle again. At the halfway mark, make a dot with a pencil.

6. Take the paper clip and straighten one end. Create a hole through the circle at the dot using the end of the paper clip.

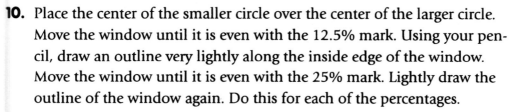

7. Divide the large circle into eight approximately equal sections by drawing four lines through the center of the circle.

8. Using the end of the paper clip again, make a hole in the center of the larger circle at the point where all the lines come together.

9. On the outside edge of the larger circle, using the lines as guides, write the following percentages: 12.5%, 25%, 37.5%, 50%, 62.5%, 75%, 87.5%, 100%.

10. Place the center of the smaller circle over the center of the larger circle. Move the window until it is even with the 12.5% mark. Using your pencil, draw an outline very lightly along the inside edge of the window. Move the window until it is even with the 25% mark. Lightly draw the outline of the window again. Do this for each of the percentages.

11. Take the smaller circle off. Write the equation $1/8 = 0.125$ inside the window you drew next to 12.5%. Now write the following equations next to the percentage that follows them:

$1/4 = 0.250 = 25\%$

$3/8 = 0.375 = 37.5\%$

$1/2 = 0.5 = 50\%$

$5/8 = 0.625 = 62.5\%$

$6/8 = 0.75 = 75\%$

$7/8 = 0.875 = 87.5\%$

$8/8 = 1.0 = 100\%$

12. Place the small circle on top of the large circle. Use a paper brad (paper fastener) to connect the two circles in the center.

13. Spin the wheel. The percentage on the outside of the wheel is equal to the fraction and decimals inside the window.

14. Use the wheel to test yourself. Can you remember the equation that should appear in the window for every percentage on the wheel?

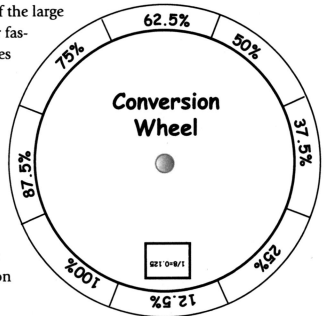

27

Colored Candy Magic

To change a fraction to a percent, divide the numerator by the denominator and multiply by 100. Practice changing fractions to percents while you figure out what percentage of a bag of colored chocolate candies is red and what percentage is other colors.

MATERIALS

2 small bags of colored chocolate candies

pencil

paper

calculator

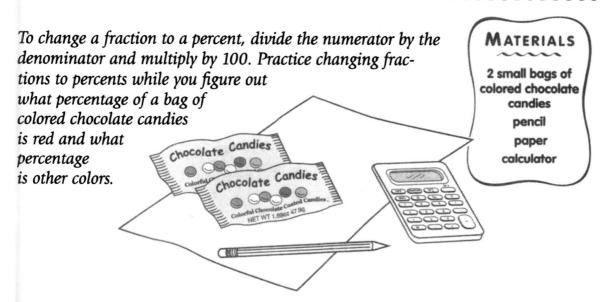

Procedure

1. Open a bag of candies. Sort the candies by color.

How many red candies are there?

How many orange candies are there?

How many yellow candies are there?

How many blue candies are there?

How many green candies are there?

How many brown candies are there?

How many candies are there all together?

Write down your answers on a piece of paper.

2. Divide the number of red candies by the total number of candies. Your answer will be a decimal. Multiply this answer by 100 to find the percentage of red candies.

For example, if you counted 22 red candies out of a total of 55 candies, you would divide 22 by 55 and get 0.40. Multiply 0.40 by 100 and you will find that 40% of the candies in the bag are red.

3. Next divide the number of orange candies by the total number of candies. Multiply this answer by 100 to find the percentage of orange candies.

4. Continue to repeat these steps with each color of candies.

5. Now eat all the red candies. How many candies are left?

What percentage of the candies is orange? (Divide the number of orange candies by the new total number of candies.)

What percentage of the candies is yellow?

What percentage of the candies is blue?

What percentage of the candies is green?

What percentage of the candies is brown?

6. Now eat all the orange candies. How many candies are left?

What percentage of the candies is yellow? (Remember to divide the number of yellow candies by the *new* total number of candies.)

What percentage of the candies is blue?

What percentage of the candies is green?

What percentage of the candies is brown?

7. Now eat all the yellow candies. How many candies are left?

What percentage of the candies is blue?

What percentage of the candies is green?

What percentage of the candies is brown?

8. Now eat all the blue candies. How many candies are left?

What percentage of the candies is green?

What percentage of the candies is brown?

9. Now eat all the green candies. Only brown candies are left. How many brown candies are left? What percentage of the candies is brown?

10. Check your math with the calculator.

11. Open the other bag of candies. Sort and count the candies in this bag.

How do they differ from the candies in your original bag?

Is there the same number of candies in each bag?

Is there the same number of candies of each color?

Make a chart like the one below to compare the two bags of candies.

NUMBER OF COLORS OF CANDIES IN EACH OF THE TWO BAGS

	Bag 1	Bag 2
Red		
Orange		
Yellow		
Blue		
Green		
Brown		
Total		

12. Now that you know the number of each color, you can calculate the percentage of each color of candies. Only by calculating the percentages can you accurately compare the two bags. Remember to calculate the percentage of each color by dividing the number of candies of that color by the total number of candies and then by multiplying the answer by 100. Enter the answers in a table like the one shown here.

Now that you have compared two bags of candies, can you draw any conclusions about candies? Are there more candies of one color in both bags? How much do the percentages of each color vary from bag to bag?

PERCENTAGE OF COLORS OF CANDIES
IN EACH OF THE TWO BAGS

	Bag 1	Bag 2
Red		
Orange		
Yellow		
Green		
Blue		
Brown		

BRAIN Stretcher

Use a pie chart to display the percentages of the colors of candies in a bag of candies. Color the chart to match the colors of the candies.

28

Juice Labels

When you are shopping for juices, you have to read labels carefully. Something that's called a "juice drink" or a "juice cocktail" doesn't have to be 100% juice. Instead, many of these drinks are mostly water and sugar. Explore the world of juice drinks as you practice finding the percentage of a whole number.

MATERIALS

pencil

paper

three different types of juice drinks (be sure it says "drink" on the label)

calculator

measuring cup

glass

APPLE DRINK

5% Juice

Great Grape Juice Drink

25% Real Grape Juice

Juicy Maid Orange Drink

10% Real Juice

1 CUP
3/4 CUP
1/2 CUP
1/4 CUP

Procedure

1. Copy the chart below on a piece of paper.

1 Name of Juice	2 Percent Juice	3 Percent Juice as a Decimal	4 Ounces in Each Drink	5 Ounces of Juice

2. Look at the bottles and/or boxes of juice drinks you have selected. Enter the names of the juice drinks in column 1 of the chart.

3. Read on the label how much juice each box or bottle of juice contains. The juice content is written as a percentage. For instance, a box of orange juice might say "Contains 12% juice." Enter your findings in column 2 of the chart.

4. Change the percentage of juice to a decimal by dividing the percentage by 100. Enter the results in column 3.

5. Read each label to find how many ounces are in each drink. Enter the results in column 4 of the chart.

6. Now multiply the results in column 3 by those in column 4 to find out the number of *ounces of juice* in each drink. Enter the results in column 5. Use the calculator for help.

7. Open one of the containers of juice. Use a measuring cup to measure the amount of juice in column 5 and pour it in a glass. This is the amount of actual juice in the entire drink.

Look at the label of the juice box or bottle to see how many calories are in the entire box or bottle of juice. Now figure out how many calories are in the selection you just poured.

Money Sleuth

How can you find out how much money someone paid for an item on sale if you know the amount saved and the percentage saved?

To find the original price of an item, divide the amount saved by the percentage of savings. Change the percent to a decimal before you divide.

EXAMPLE

If a stereo is reduced $20, or 10%, what is the original price of the stereo?

$$\$20 \div 10\% = \$20 \div 0.10 = \$200$$

The original price was $200.

To find the sale price, subtract the savings from the original price.

$$\$200 - \$20 = \$180$$

The sale price is $180.

Game Preparation

Each player writes the following problem on a sheet of paper.

I bought a _____.

It was ____% off.

I saved $____.

How much was the item originally?

What was the sale price of the item?

Game Rules

1. Players look in the newspapers for an ad that lists items on sale. Each player fills in the blanks in the word problem with the information in an ad. (You may have to calculate the amount of savings if the ad only gives a percentage and the sale price.)

2. The two players exchange problems and solve them. The player who correctly solves the problem first is the winner.

VI

PERCENTS IN EVERYDAY LIFE

Percents are one of the most useful mathematical concepts you'll ever learn. In this section you'll put your knowledge of percents to good use. You'll learn how to figure out how much the sales tax would be on a purchase, and how to create a tipping chart so that you know how much of a tip to leave at a restaurant. You'll also learn how interest works in a bank account, and you'll determine what the chance is of rolling a certain number with two dice.

From State to State

Many U.S. states put a sales tax on various items. Each state has a different tax rate, which is expressed as a percentage. In this activity you'll use the Internet to find the amount of sales tax in different states and then figure out what the same items would cost, including tax, in different states. To make things even more complicated, some cities add a city sales tax to purchases in addition to the state sales tax.

MATERIALS

computer with Internet access
pencil
paper

Procedure

1. Log on to the Internet.

2. Find the sales tax in each state by entering the state name and "sales tax" in a search engine. Write your findings on a piece of paper.

3. Five states have no sales tax. What are they?

4. Mississippi and Rhode Island have the highest sales tax in the United States. What is the rate of sales tax in these states?

5. In what state do you live? What is the state sales tax there?

6. What is the average state sales tax in the United States? (*Hint:* Add the sales taxes for all 50 states and divide by 50.)

7. If you bought the following items in the following states, how much state sales tax would you have to pay? (*Hint:* Change the tax rate to a decimal and multiply by the price of the item.)

	Soft Drink $1	Blue Jeans $35	Television $500
Alaska			
Hawaii			
Illinois			
New York			
Rhode Island			

BRAIN Stretcher

Use the Internet to find out if there is sales tax in other countries. Pick any three countries and use a search engine to find the sales tax in those countries.

SUPER BRAIN Stretcher

Different cities like New York add city sales tax to different items. How much tax would be added to the purchase of a $300 stereo in Albany, New York; Buffalo, New York; and New York, New York? Look up city tax rates on the Internet to find out.

Here's a Tip

MATERIALS

pencil
index card
calculator

Use your knowledge of figuring out percentages of whole numbers to make a tipping chart. Take your tipping chart to a restaurant so that you can tell one of your parents how much tip to leave your server.

Procedure

1. Copy the following chart on an index card.

Cost of Food	Fair Service (10% Tip)	Average Service (15% Tip)	Excellent Service (20% Tip)
$5	$0.50	$0.75	$1.00
$10	$1.00	$1.50	
$15			
$20		$3.00	
$25	$2.50		$5.00
$30			
$35		$5.25	
$40		$6.00	

2. Fill in the missing values using the Tips and Tricks section for help.

3. To use the tipping chart, find the total price of the meal in the left-hand column. Round up the price to the nearest $5. If the bill was $27.50, round the bill up to $30 and find the appropriate tip for that amount. If the service was fair, leave a 10% tip; if the service was average, leave a 15% tip; and if the service was exceptional, leave a 20% tip. Carry the tipping chart in your wallet. The next time you and your family go to a restaurant, use the chart to figure out how much of a tip to leave the server.

Tips and Tricks

To find how much a 10% tip should be on a specific bill, first change 10% to a decimal (0.10), then multiply 0.10 by the amount of the bill.

Example

What is a 10% tip on a $16 bill?

$$0.10 \times 16 = \$1.60$$

To find how much a 15% tip should be on a specific bill, first change 15% to a decimal (0.15), then multiply 0.15 by the amount of the bill.

Example

What is a 15% tip on a $16 bill?

$$0.15 \times 16 = \$2.40$$

To find how much a 20% tip should be on a specific bill, first change 20% to a decimal (0.20), then multiply 0.20 by the amount of the bill.

Example

What is a 20% tip on a $16 bill?

$$0.20 \times 16 = \$3.20$$

Get a take-out menu and have the members of your family pretend to order what they would like to have. Add up the cost of the items your family selected. Round up to the nearest $5 and look on your tip chart to see what the tip should be, assuming you had excellent service.

Interested in Money?

If you deposit your money in a savings account, the bank pays you a percentage of your deposit while your money stays there. The money the bank pays you is called interest and the percentage is the interest rate. The more money you deposit, the more interest you earn. There are two basic kinds of interest: simple and compound. With simple interest, you only earn interest on your initial investment. With compound interest, you earn interest on your initial investment plus interest on the previous interest earned. This activity will show you how to calculate bank interest, which is always expressed as a percentage.

Procedure

1. Copy the chart on page 93 on a piece of paper.

2. Assume your account earns 5% simple interest per year. Using a calculator, compute the interest earned in one year on a $100 initial investment by multiplying $0.05 \times \$100$. The result is $5. You would earn $5 per year in simple interest. Every year your investment would increase by $5. So

Time	Simple Interest (5%)	Compound Interest (5%)	Simple Interest (10%)	Compound Interest (10%)
Starting amount	$100	$100	$100	$100
½ year				
1 year	$105		$110	
2 years				
3 years				
4 years				
5 years				
10 years	$150		$200	
20 years				
100 years				

after one year, your investment would be worth $105 and after 10 years it would be worth $150. Calculate what your investment would be after a half year up to 100 years. Fill in the second column of the chart.

3. Now assume your account earns 10% simple interest per year. Compute the interest earned in one year on a $100 initial investment by multiplying 0.1 × $100. The result is $10. You would earn $10 per year in simple interest. Every year your investment would increase by $10. So after one year, your investment would be worth $110 and after 10 years it would be worth $200. Fill in the fourth column of the chart.

4. Now assume your account earns 5% compound interest per year. To calculate how much your initial investment of $100 would earn at this rate, we're going to use a compound interest calculator on the Internet. Log on to the Internet and go to the website www.mathwizz.com. Click on the link to the compound interest calculator.

5. Where it says, *How much do you want to invest?*, enter 100.

6. Where it says, *Enter the annual interest rate,* enter 5.

7. Now enter the time, *1 year.*

8. Where it says, *How often do you want the interest compounded?*, enter daily.

9. Click *Find the total amount saved*. The computer will compute results for you. Enter the results in the chart.

10. Complete the third column of the chart by entering the different times indicated.

11. In the compound interest calculator, change the annual interest rate to 10% and enter the different times from the chart. Fill in the results in the fifth column of the chart.

12. How much more money would you make after 100 years with compound interest at 5% than with simple interest at 5%? How much more would you make with compound interest at 10%?

BRAIN Stretcher

How much money would you have if you put an entire year's allowance in a bank and didn't withdraw it until you were 21 years old? To figure it out, follow these steps:

1. How much allowance do you get a week?

2. If you saved your allowance for a year, how much would you have? (Multiply your weekly allowance by 52.)

3. How long will it be until you are 21 years old? (Subtract your age from 21 years.)

4. How much interest does a savings account at your local bank offer?

5. Now pretend you put this year's allowance in the bank and didn't touch it until you were 21 years old. How much money would you have? Use the compound interest calculator to figure out the answer.

Better Deal

To find the sale price of an item, follow these three steps:

MATERIALS

newspaper
and/or
computer with
Internet access

pencil

paper

1. *Change the sale amount from a percentage to a decimal.*
2. *Multiply the decimal by the amount of the item to find the dollar amount of the discount.*
3. *Subtract the discount from the original price to find the sale price.*

EXAMPLE

If the original price is $15 and it is 40% off, what is the sale price?
    First, change the sale amount from a percentage to a decimal.
40% is 0.4
    Second, multiply the decimal by the amount of the item.
$0.4 \times \$15.00 = \$6.00$
    Finally, subtract the discount from the original price to find the sale price.
$\$15.00 - \$6.00 = \$9.00$

Try this activity to find out if a bigger percentage off is always the best deal.

Procedure

1. Go through the newspaper or browse the Internet to find advertisements for identical items that are on sale at different percentages off and write them down. Be sure the ad lists the item's original price as well.

2. Determine the discounted price of the item at each store.

3. Which store gives you the better deal? Is it always the store that offers the highest percentage off?

Health Watch

*Use your knowledge of percents to determine your
daily calorie, fat, and carbohydrate intake.*

MATERIALS

pencil
paper
calorie guide

Procedure

1. Copy the chart below on a piece of paper
and use it to keep a log of everything
you eat or drink in a single day,
including specific quanti-
ties (such as $^1/_2$ cup
of cereal, $^1/_4$ pound
hamburger).

2. Look up the number of calories, grams of fat, and grams of carbohydrates in each of the foods you ate. Enter
the results in the chart. You can find this
information in a calorie book at your local library
or at www.caloriecountercharts.com.

3. Add up the number of calories, grams of fat, and grams of carbohydrates
you ate in a single day.

4. Each gram of fat has 9 calories and each gram of carbohydrates has 4
calories. What percentage of your daily calories came from fat? What percentage of your daily calories came from carbohydrates?

Food and Quantity	Calories	Grams of Fat	Grams of Carbohydrates
Breakfast			
Lunch			
Dinner			
Snacks			
Total			

Game of Chance

When you roll a pair of dice, do you have the same chance of rolling every number from 2 to 12? Try this activity to find out.

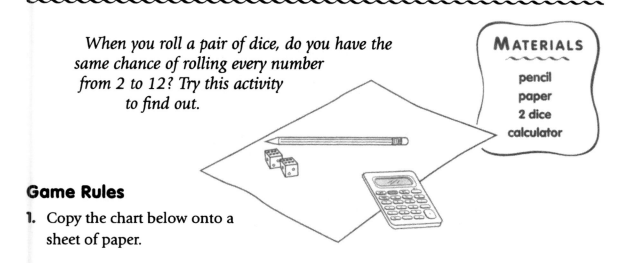

Game Rules

1. Copy the chart below onto a sheet of paper.

	2	3	4	5	6	7	8	9	10	11	12
10 Rolls											
Percentage											
25 Rolls											
Percentage											
100 Rolls											
Percentage											
Ways to Roll Numbers											
Percentage											

2. Roll two dice. Add the numbers showing on the dice together and enter the total in the chart by putting a slash mark [/] in the correct column.

3. Now roll the dice nine more times and enter results in the chart each time.

4. Use the calculator to compute the percentage of the time you rolled each of the numbers from 2 to 12. Enter the results in the chart. (Use the Tips and Tricks section for help.)

5. Now roll the dice 25 times. How many times did you roll each number? Enter the results in the chart.

6. What percentage of the time did you roll each of the numbers from 2 to 12? Enter the results in the chart. Use the calculator for help. (Use the Tips and Tricks section for more help.)

7. Now roll the dice 100 times. How many times did you roll each number? Enter the results in the chart.

8. What percentage of the time did you roll each of the numbers from 2 to 12? Enter the results in the chart. Use the calculator for help. (Use the Tips and Tricks section for more help.)

9. Compare your results. Were there differences depending on how many times you rolled the dice?

Get a red die and a black die and use them to figure out how many different ways there are to roll each of the numbers from 2 to 12.

Here's some help to get you started.

When you roll two dice, there are 36 different possible rolls. What are they?

There is only one way to roll a 2 using two dice:

> A 1 on the red die and a 1 on the black die

There are only two ways to roll a 3 using two dice:

> A 1 on the red die and a 2 on the black die
>
> A 2 on the red die and a 1 on the black die

The are six ways to roll a 7 using two dice:

> A 6 on the red die and a 1 on the black die
>
> A 5 on the red die and a 2 on the black die
>
> A 4 on the red die and a 3 on the black die
>
> A 3 on the red die and a 4 on the black die
>
> A 2 on the red die and a 5 on the black die
>
> A 1 on the red die and a 6 on the black die

What is the chance of rolling each of the numbers?

(*Hint:* Divide the number of ways to roll a number by 36.)

Tips and Tricks

When you roll the dice 10 times, you just need to multiply the number of times a number came up by 10 to find the percentage of time each number was rolled.

Example

If you rolled the number 5 three times, then 5 was rolled 30% of the time: $3 \times 10 = 30$.

Why? You rolled the same number 3 out of 10 times, which is $\frac{3}{10}$ or 0.3 of the time. Multiply 0.3×100 to get 30%.

When you roll the dice 25 times, you just need to multiply the number of times a number came up by 4 to find the percentage of time each number was rolled.

Example

If you rolled the number 5 three times, then 5 was rolled 12% of the time: $3 \times 4 = 12\%$.

Why? You rolled the same number 3 out of 25 times, which is $\frac{3}{25}$ or 0.12 of the time. Multiply 0.12×100 to get 12%.

When you rolled the dice 100 times, the number of times you roll each number is the same as the percentage of times you roll each number.

Example

If you rolled the number 5 three times, then you rolled the number 3% of the time.

Why? You rolled the same number 3 out of 100 times, which is $\frac{3}{100}$ or 0.03 of the time. Multiply 0.03×100 to get 3%.

36

Commercial Time

Figure out what percentage of your favorite TV show is taken up by commercials.

MATERIALS

pencil
paper
television
clock or watch

Procedure

1. Have a pencil and paper handy when your favorite TV show comes on. Make a note of how long the show is supposed to be, such as 30 minutes or 60 minutes.

2. Every time there is a commercial break, time how long it lasts.

3. When the show is over, add up the total number of minutes of commercials.

4. Divide the number of minutes of commercial time by the total time for the show. Multiply the answer by 100. The result is the percentage of time during your show that you spent watching commercials.

~~~VII~~~
WRAP IT UP!

Now that you know everything about fractions, decimals, and percents, here are a few fun reviews to keep your skills sharp. In this section you can practice by playing Math Review Game, creating your own crazy problems, solving crossword puzzles, and making goofy "math lib" stories.

Math Review Game

Play this game with a friend to review your decimal, fraction, and percent facts.

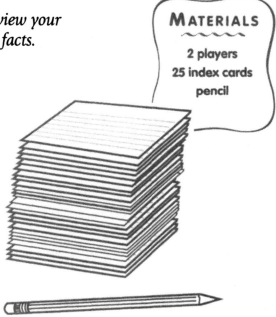

MATERIALS

2 players
25 index cards
pencil

Game Preparation

1. On the back of five index cards, write "Decimals and Percents."

2. On the back of five index cards, write "Fractions and Decimals."

3. On the back of five index cards, write "Fractions and Percents."

4. On the back of five index cards, write "Addition and Subtraction of Decimals and Percents."

5. On the back of five index cards, write "Multiplication and Division of Decimals and Percents."

6. Below the words on each set of cards, write one of the following numbers on each card: 10, 20, 30, 40, or 50. For example, in the decimals and percents set, one card should have a 10, one a 20, one a 30, one a 40, and one a 50. A sample card is shown here.

Decimals and Percents

10

Game Rules

1. Shuffle the cards and deal them out to the players. There are 25 cards, so one player gets 12 cards and the other gets 13.

2. Players create problems and write one problem on the front of each of their cards.

The category labeled on the back of the card determines the type of problem. For example, on the card that is labeled "Fractions and Decimals, 10 points," a player might write the problem *Change ¹/₂ to a decimal.*

The number on the back of the card, which is the number of points earned for correctly answering the problem, determines the difficulty level of the problem on that card. Cards with higher numbers should have more difficult problems, while cards with lower numbers should have easier problems.

3. Once all of the problems have been written, the players place all the cards on the table so that the problems are facedown. Arrange the cards in five columns according to category and five rows according to point value. Put

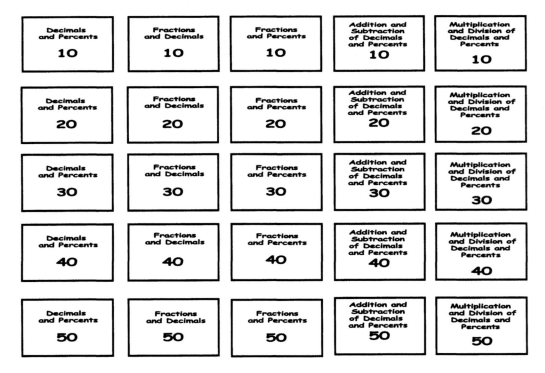

the "Decimals and Percents" in the first column, the "Fractions and Decimals" in the second column, and so on. Put the 10-point cards in row 1, the 20-point cards in row 2, the 30-point cards in row 3, the 40-point cards in row 4, and the 50-point cards in row 5.

4. Player 1 turns over any card, and both players try to solve the problem. The first player to correctly solve the problem keeps the card and turns over another card. Both players try to solve this new problem. If a player solves a problem incorrectly, that player must give one of the cards he or she has won, of equal or greater value, to the other player. If a player has not won any cards, he or she does not have to give a card to the other player.

5. The game continues until all cards have been played. At the end of the game, players add up the points on the back of their cards to see who has won this round of Math Review Game.

Problem Generator

*Create crazy problems to practice
solving percent problems.*

Game Rules

1. Cut a sheet of colored paper into eight pieces.

2. Write one of the following percents on each piece of paper:

1%	50%
10%	80%
20%	100%
25%	250%

3. Fold each piece of paper in half and place in the bowl.

4. Cut up a different colored piece of paper into eight sections. Write one of the following numbers on each piece of paper:

$\frac{1}{2}$	75
3	100
32	1,000
50	20,000

5. Fold each of these pieces of paper in half and place them in the bowl.

6. Finally, cut up a third sheet of colored paper into eight sections. Write one of the following subjects on each piece of paper:

Dinosaurs	Potato chips
Mice	Computer games
Cactus	Tennis shoes
Soccer	Mosquitoes

7. Fold each of these pieces of paper in half and place them in the bowl.

8. Each player picks three pieces of different-colored paper from the bowl. Each player will have picked a percent, a number, and a subject.

9. On a white sheet of paper each player writes a funny math problem using all three picked items. For example, a player picks 10%, 50, and dinosaurs. His or her problem might read: 10% of a herd of dinosaurs like to play checkers. If the herd has 50 dinosaurs, how many of the dinosaurs play checkers?

10. Players exchange the created problems and solve them. Players then read the problems and their answers aloud.

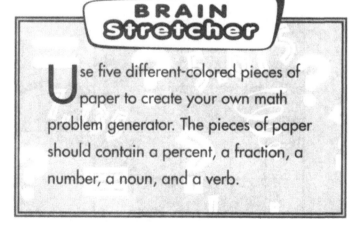

BRAIN Stretcher

Use five different-colored pieces of paper to create your own math problem generator. The pieces of paper should contain a percent, a fraction, a number, a noun, and a verb.

39

Number Cross Puzzle

Review fractions, decimals, and percents while solving this number cross puzzle.

Procedure

1. Copy the puzzle below.

2. Solve the following percent problems and write the correct answers in the spaces on the puzzle. Decimal points, percent signs, and slash signs all take up a single space and there are no zeros before decimals less than one.

Across

1. Write 89% as a decimal.
3. Write $1/2$ as a decimal.
5. Write $3/4$ as a decimal.
8. Write 50% as a decimal.
9. Write $1/5$ as a decimal.

11. Write $2^1/2$ as a percent.
12. Write 6% as a decimal.
14. Write 30% as a decimal.
15. Write $13/20$ as a decimal.
17. Write 150% as a decimal.

Down

2. Write .81 as a percent.
4. Write $5^1/2$ as a decimal.
5. Write $1/20$ as a decimal.
6. Write 0.05 as a percent.
7. Write 1 as a percent.

10. Write .4 as a fraction.
11. Write 0.02 as a percent.
12. Write 30.5% as a decimal.
13. Write 650% as a decimal.
16. Write $1/20$ as a percent.

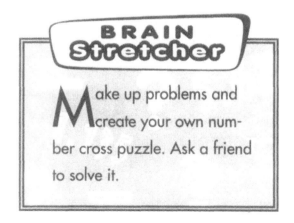

BRAIN Stretcher

Make up problems and create your own number cross puzzle. Ask a friend to solve it.

Answers to Number Cross Puzzle

1. .	2. 8	9		3. .	4. 5		5. .	7	6. 5
	1		7. 1		8. .	5	0		%
	%		0		5		5		
			0					9. .	10. 2
11. 2	5	0	%		12. .	0	13. 6		/
%				14. .	3		15. .	6	5
	16. 5				0		5		
	%		17. 1	.	5				

40

Math Libs

I'm sure you've done Mad Libs before, where you pick different kinds of words to make up a zany story. This time you'll fill in the blanks with facts about percents and decimals.

Procedure

1. Copy the story below onto a piece of paper.

2. Fill in your name and your friend's name in the blank spaces noted.

3. Ask your friend to give numbers and names to fill in the rest of the blanks. Don't let your friend see the story. Just ask him or her to give you an answer to the phrases below the blanks. For example, you might ask for a number between 0 and 100 and your friend might say 88. Write down your friend's answers.

4. When all the blanks have been filled in, read the story back to your friend and have a laugh at the story you both created.

_____ and _____ decided to head out
　　　(friend's name)　　　　　　　(your name)

on an adventure. As they were walking out the front door, they heard the meteorologist on the TV announce that there is a

_____ percent chance of snow. Impossible,
(number between 0 and 100)

they thought. It was August _____! The two
(number between 30 and 50)

friends decided to go on a shopping spree. They had

$ _____ between them. They took
(number between 1 and 1,000)

_____ to the store, and on the way to the store
(method of transportation)

they passed _____ and _____.
(name of friend)   (name of pet)

At the store everything was on sale for _____%
(number between 0 and 100)

off! Wow! They decided to buy a _____. It
(something you want)

originally cost $_____, but on sale it cost
(number between 1 and 1,000)

$_____. A bargain!
(number between 1 and 1,000)

BRAIN Stretcher

Now create your own Math Libs story that includes a decimal or percent problem.

DECIMALS AND PERCENTS MASTER CERTIFICATE

Now that you have mastered all of the problems, games, and activities in this book, you are officially certified as a decimals and percents master. Make a photocopy of this certificate, write your name on the copy, and hang it on the wall.

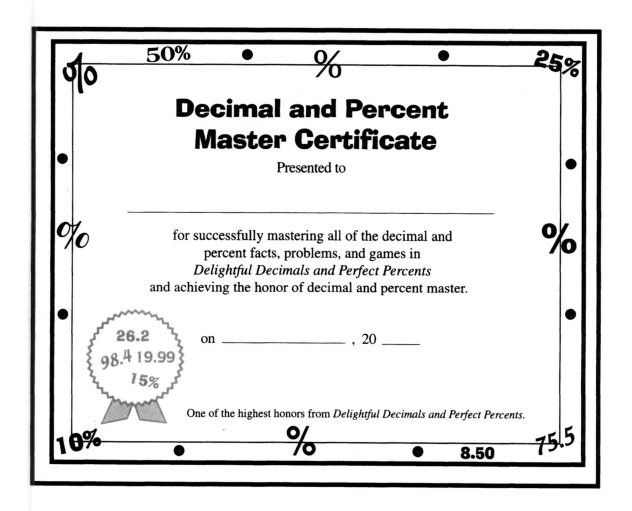

Decimal and Percent Master Certificate

Presented to

_____

for successfully mastering all of the decimal and
percent facts, problems, and games in
Delightful Decimals and Perfect Percents
and achieving the honor of decimal and percent master.

on _____ , 20 _____

One of the highest honors from *Delightful Decimals and Perfect Percents*.

Index

CPSIA information can be obtained at www.ICGtesting.com
Printed in the USA
LVOW111248170812

294661LV00005B/42/P